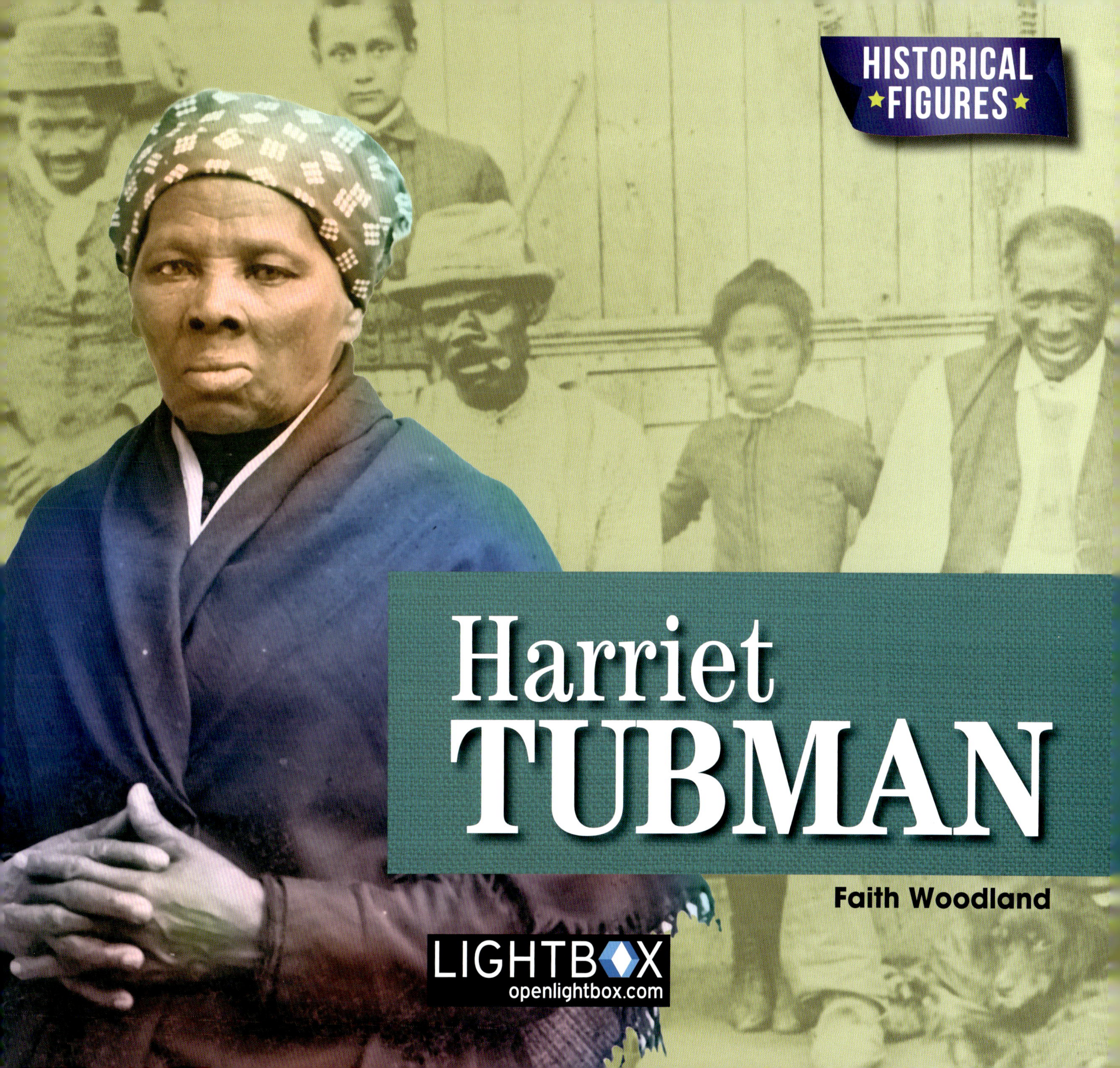
HISTORICAL FIGURES
Harriet TUBMAN
Faith Woodland
LIGHTBOX
openlightbox.com

LIGHTBOX

Go to **www.openlightbox.com** and enter this book's unique code.

ACCESS CODE

LBXW7247

Lightbox is an all-inclusive digital solution for the teaching and learning of curriculum topics in an original, groundbreaking way. Lightbox is based on National Curriculum Standards.

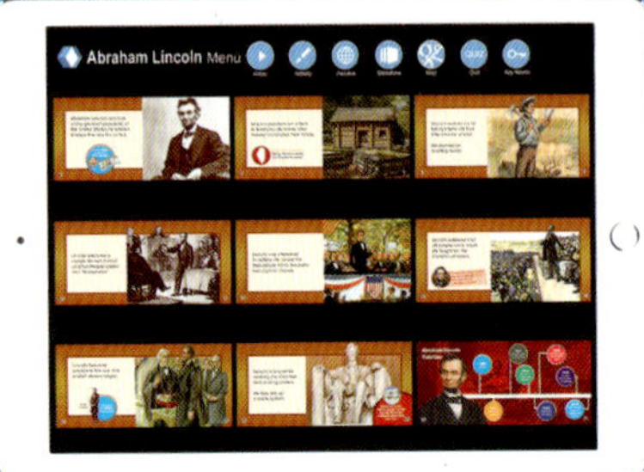

OPTIMIZED FOR

- ✓ **TABLETS**
- ✓ **WHITEBOARDS**
- ✓ **COMPUTERS**
- ✓ **AND MUCH MORE!**

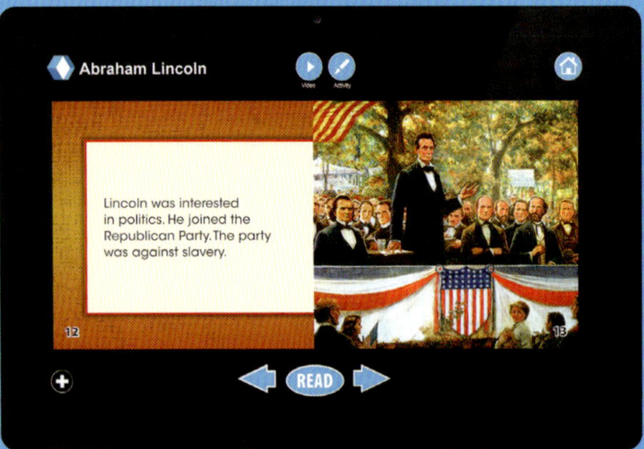

STANDARD FEATURES OF LIGHTBOX

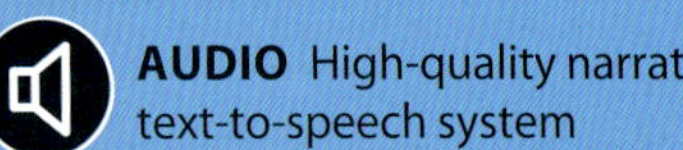
AUDIO High-quality narration using text-to-speech system

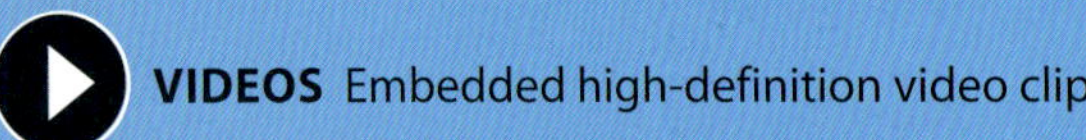
VIDEOS Embedded high-definition video clips

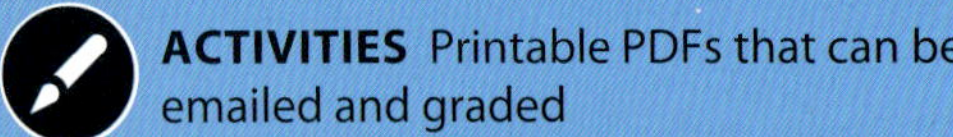
ACTIVITIES Printable PDFs that can be emailed and graded

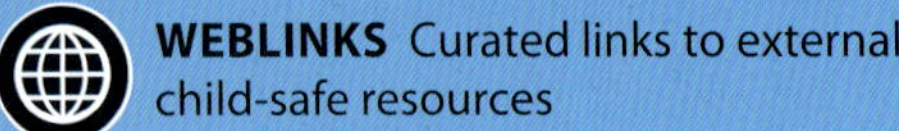
WEBLINKS Curated links to external, child-safe resources

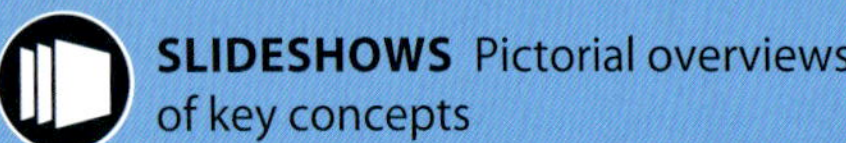
SLIDESHOWS Pictorial overviews of key concepts

INTERACTIVE MAPS Interactive maps and aerial satellite imagery

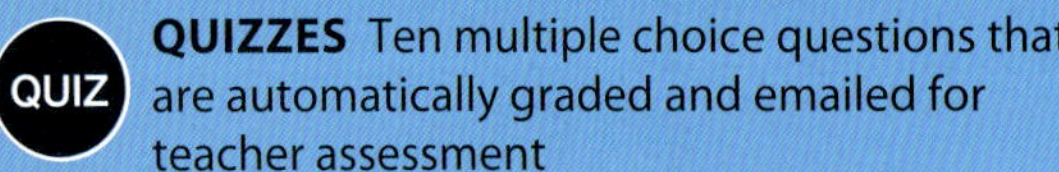
QUIZZES Ten multiple choice questions that are automatically graded and emailed for teacher assessment

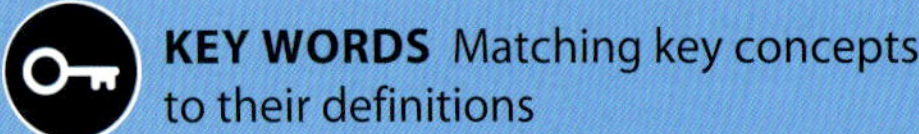
KEY WORDS Matching key concepts to their definitions

VIDEOS

WEBLINKS

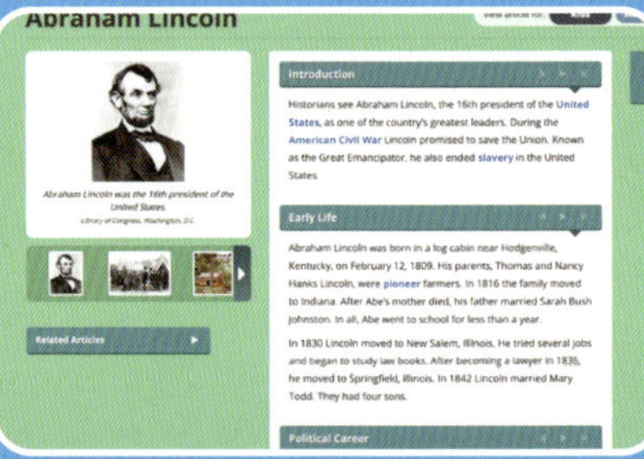

SLIDESHOWS

QUIZZES

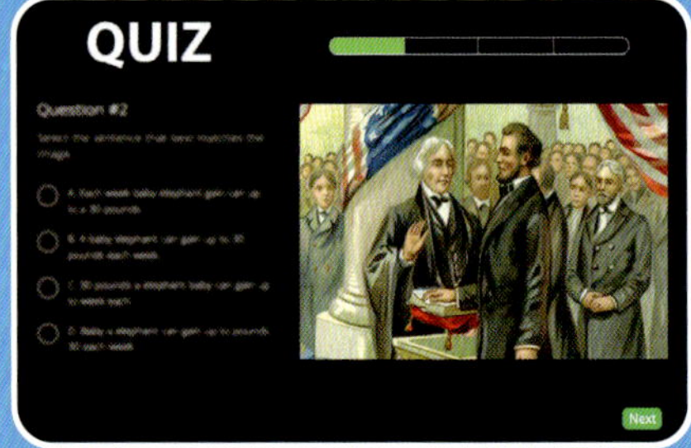

Harriet TUBMAN

Contents

Harriet Tubman was born a slave, but escaped. She helped many other slaves escape, too.

Tubman was born in Maryland. Her name was Araminta Ross.

She had eight siblings. Some of them were sold to other slaveowners.

Tubman returned to Maryland 19 times to help more slaves escape.

7

Tubman had to work as a maid and a cook. It was very hard.

Tubman ran away from her owners. She walked 90 miles to Philadelphia to be free.

Tubman was an abolitionist. This means that she worked to end slavery.

There was a secret path called the Underground Railroad. Slaves used it to escape from the South to the North. Tubman led many slaves to freedom along this path.

Tubman believed in helping others. She wanted to change the world for the better.

"I prayed to God to make me strong and able to fight, and that's what I've always prayed for ever since."
– Harriet Tubman

There was a war between the North and South. Tubman worked as a cook and a spy for the North.

Tubman was part of a raid that **freed 700 slaves.**

Tubman showed at least 70 other slaves how to use the Underground Railroad on their own.

She is remembered as a brave woman.

Tubman started the **Harriet Tubman Home for Aged and Indigent Negroes** in **Auburn, New York.**

Harriet Tubman Timeline

1849
Escapes to the North

1874
Adopts a daughter named Gertie

1857
Helps her parents escape

1913
Dies

1869
Marries Nelson Davis

2019
The movie *Harriet* is released in theaters

Cause

A cause is the reason something happens.

Tubman was forced to work as a slave.

Tubman believed all people should live freely.

Effect

An effect is the outcome.

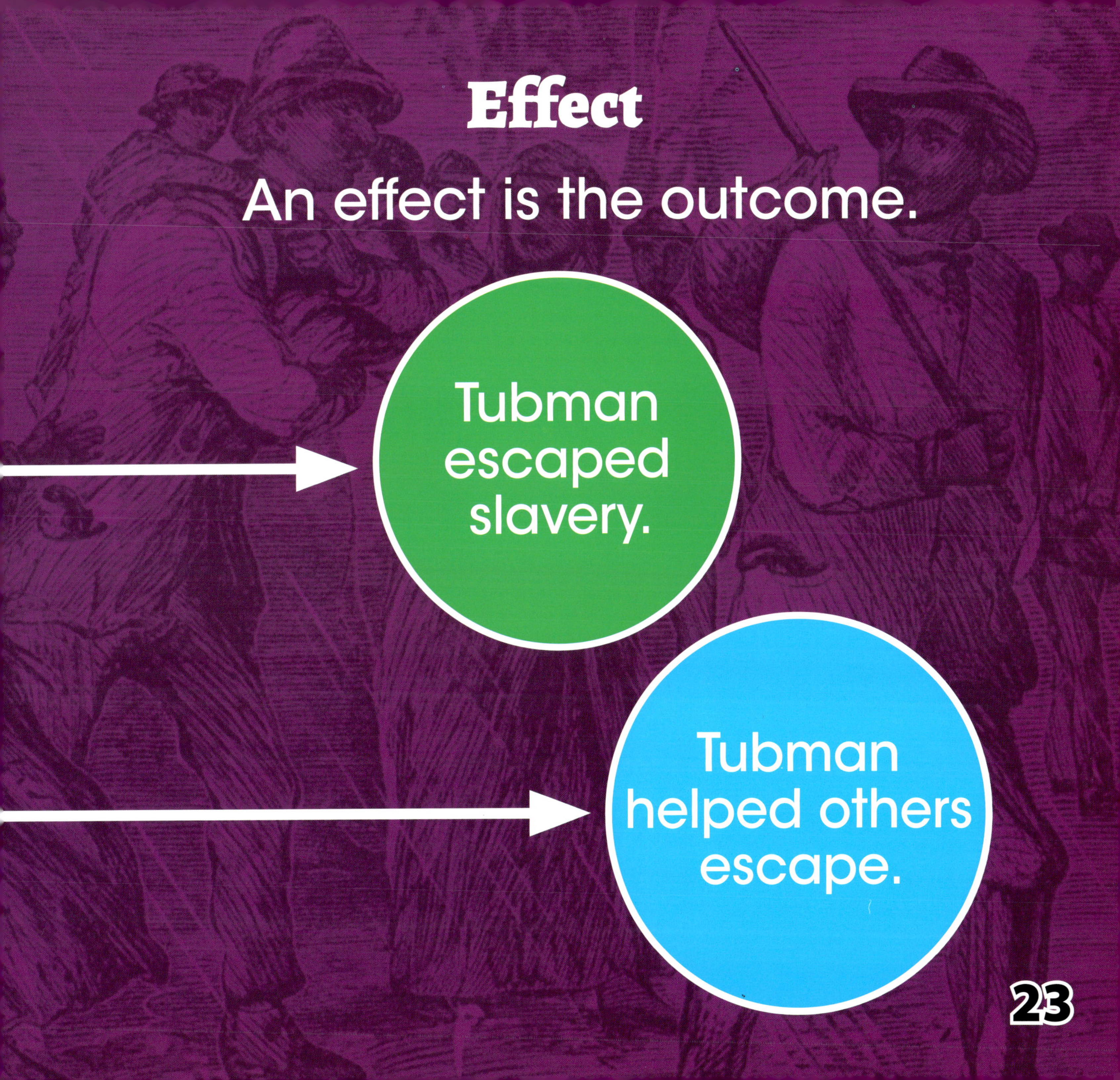

KEY WORDS

Research has shown that as much as 65 percent of all written material published in English is made up of 300 words. These 300 words cannot be taught using pictures or learned by sounding them out. They must be recognized by sight. This book contains 65 common sight words to help young readers improve their reading fluency and comprehension. This book also teaches young readers several important content words, such as proper nouns. These words are paired with pictures to aid in learning and improve understanding.

Page	Sight Words First Appearance
4	a, but, many, more, other, she, than, to, too, was
6	had, help, her, in, name, of, some, them, times, were
8	and, as, away, be, from, hard, it, miles, very, walked, work
10	an, end, means, that, this
12	along, the, there
14	always, change, ever, for, I, make, me, what, world
16	between, part
18	at, how, is, on, own, their, use
19	home, new, started
22	all, live, people, should, something

Page	Content Words First Appearance
4	Harriet Tubman, safety, slave
6	Araminta Ross, Maryland, siblings, slaveowners
8	cook, maid, owners, Philadelphia
10	abolitionist, slavery
12	freedom, North, path, South, Underground Railroad
14	God
16	cook, raid, spy, war
18	woman
19	Auburn, Harriet Tubman Home for Aged and Indigent Negroes, New York
20	John Tubman, timeline
21	daughter, Gertie, movie, Nelson Davis, parents, theaters
22	cause, reason
23	effect, outcome

Published by Smartbook Media Inc.
350 5th Avenue, 59th Floor New York, NY 10118
Website: www.openlightbox.com

Library of Congress Cataloging-in-Publication Data

Names: Woodland, Faith, author.
Title: Harriet Tubman / Faith Woodland.
Description: New York : Lightbox, 2020. | Series: Historical figures | Audience: Ages 4-8 | Audience: Grades K-1
Identifiers: LCCN 2020014266 (print) | LCCN 2020014267 (ebook) | ISBN 9781510553668 (library binding) | ISBN 9781510553675 | ISBN 9781510553682
Subjects: LCSH: Tubman, Harriet, 1822-1913--Juvenile literature. | Slaves--United States--Biography--Juvenile literature. | African American women--Biography--Juvenile literature. | Underground Railroad--Juvenile literature.
Classification: LCC E444.T82 W66 2020 (print) | LCC E444.T82 (ebook) | DDC 973.7/115092 [B]--dc23
LC record available at https://lccn.loc.gov/2020014266
LC ebook record available at https://lccn.loc.gov/2020014267

Printed in Guangzhou, China
1 2 3 4 5 6 7 8 9 0 24 23 22 21 20

042020
110819

Project Coordinator: Priyanka Das
Designer: Ana María Vidal

Every reasonable effort has been made to trace ownership and to obtain permission to reprint copyright material. The publisher would be pleased to have any errors or omissions brought to its attention so that they may be corrected in subsequent printings.

The publisher acknowledges Alamy, iStock, and Getty Images as the primary image suppliers for this title.